PLACE-NAMES

Also in this series

ROBERT BURNS

CLANS AND TARTANS

MARY QUEEN OF SCOTS

MYSTERIES AND LEGENDS

WILDLIFE

BONNIE PRINCE CHARLIE

CASTLES

FOOD AND DRINK

RAILWAYS

SCOTCH WHISKY

EDINBURGH

Series editor KENNETH BAILEY
Design by WESTPOINT
Cover photograph by courtesy of James W Murray

© SPURBOOKS 1982
Published by SPURBOOKS (a division of Holmes McDougall Ltd),
Allander House, 137 Leith Walk, Edinburgh EH6 8NS

Printed in Great Britain by Holmes McDougall Ltd, Edinburgh
ISBN 0 7157 2086 4

PLACE NAMES

Fiona Johnstone

Drawings by Catriona Millar

Spurbooks

CONTENTS

INTRODUCTION

THE place-names of Scotland can be a great source of interest and amusement to visitors to Scotland and, indeed, to many native Scots. The tourist in Scotland may be struck by the unusual sound or spelling of a place-name, and is often baffled by its pronunciation. Names whose present-day spellings no longer resemble their pronunciation, such as Milngavie (Mulguy) and Culross (Cooross), and names which seem calculated simply to twist the tongue of an English-speaker, such as Auchtermuchty and Drumnadrochit, are to be found in abundance.

A knowledge of the basic elements of place-names in Scotland, and an understanding of their origins, can add to the visitor's enjoyment and appreciation of the places he or she visits. A long car or bus journey can even be enlivened for all the family by playing games with place-names; by searching, for instance, for different elements in names, such as 'inver', 'achna' and 'bal' on roadsigns.

For Scottish people themselves, the interest of Scottish place-names may go a little deeper than this, since their study can reveal a great deal about Scotland's linguistic and social history. Long dead industries are remembered in the names of Leadhills in Strathclyde, where leadmines flourished, and Prestonpans in Lothian, where salt-pans were constructed to make sea-salt. The name of Bettyhill in Sutherland evokes the memory of the Highland Clearances, since it was a village built purely for the purpose of re-housing evicted crofters, and was named, rather inappropriately, perhaps, after Elizabeth, Countess of Sutherland, whose family had been the cause of their eviction.

THE LANGUAGES

Scotland's place-names have a certain mystery about them, a fascination which stems largely from the fact that many of them are still in Gaelic, that language which is now spoken only by a small percentage of the population of Scotland. Gaelic, of course, was once spoken over much of the mainland of Scotland, extending right over to the east coast, far beyond its present limits in the north-west and Western Isles. And an examination of the Gaelic place-names of Scotland reveals that these strange and perhaps rather romantic-sounding names are in fact very clear, precise descriptions of the place and its topography.

Drumnadrochit, for instance, means 'ridge of the bridge' from the Gaelic *druim*, meaning 'back' or 'ridge' and *drochaid* – 'bridge', a fair description of the location of this village near Loch Ness. A glance at an Ordnance Survey map of any of the mountainous areas of Northern Scotland shows that many of the mountain names are simply descriptions in Gaelic of the mountain's appearance and geography. Cairngorm, to take a well-known example, is 'green-blue hill' from Gaelic *carn* – 'hill' and *gorm* – 'green-blue'.

Well over half of Scotland's place-names are Gaelic in origin, although in many cases the influence of English has altered their pronunciation dramatically. A prime example of this is the village of King Edward, in Grampian, which at first glance would appear to be a memorial in name to King Edward I, the 'Hammer of the Scots', or to one of the more recent kings of this name, or even, given the rural setting of the village, to a type of potato! But no. It is actually derived from the Gaelic *cinn eadaradh*, meaning 'at the head of the division', and must be one of the earliest examples of this phenomenon of folk-etymology, since it has been known under this name for some 600 years. It is interesting to note, however, that the local pronunciation is 'Kinedart', which is much closer to the original Gaelic, and seems to indicate that the influence of English was much stronger in the written than in the spoken language.

It should not be assumed, however, that Gaelic is the key to all Scottish place-names. Far from it. From earliest times, until the Middle Ages, there took place a complex layering of different languages throughout Scotland. When, where and how all the different languages were used is still a subject of scholarly dispute, and any brief explanation must be a simplification, perhaps an over-simplification. The languages can, nevertheless, be broken down into six basic categories.

The pre-Celtic language

This language cannot really be identified, and is effectively a means of explaining a few names which defy analysis. River names, in particular, tend to preserve remnants of older languages, and in Scotland there are many river names – Nevis, Nairn, Tay, Affric and so on – which cannot be explained except in terms of an ancient pre-Celtic language which is no longer decipherable, 7 because it seems to have been totally unrelated to the Celtic, Scandinavian or Anglo-Saxon languages still known to us. Links between the names of various rivers in Europe have been suggested; Tay/Thames/Tamar/Teviot may stem from one common pre-Celtic river name, but this is not of great relevance to Scottish place-names in particular, and for this reason, discussion of these ancient river names has been kept to a minimum in this book.

Brittonic or P-Celtic

This is the earliest identifiable language-group in Scotland, and is closely related to present-day Welsh, Breton and Cornish. It was certainly spoken by Britons in the old kingdom of Strathclyde in the south-west before the third century. It is also thought to have been spoken in a different dialect by the Picts, although exactly who the Picts were and in which areas they lived, is not at all clear. There is more evidence of their presence in the north and east of Scotland than elsewhere, and in these areas, inscriptions on standing-stones and crosses give us some evidence of their existence, if nothing else. It is said that when St Columba, an Irish-Gaelic speaker, visited a Pictish king at Inverness in the seventh century, they could not communicate at all, and the Venerable Bede, writing in the eighth century, seemed to regard Pictish as a totally separate language from Brittonic, Gaelic or English. It has been suggested that there were in fact two separate Pictish languages, one pre-Celtic and one Brittonic, which would explain the apparent links with Brittonic, and the differences. This is not certain, however, and may perhaps never be certain, given the shadowy presence of the Picts in history.

Gaelic or Q-Celtic

This name covers Irish, Scottish and Manx Gaelic as we know them today, and this type of Gaelic had virtually supplanted Brittonic by the eighth century as a result of migrations from Ireland by the original Scots, and the influence of the Celtic church, led by St Columba. It did, of course, continue to develop and change as languages do, over the years, creating different dialects, in particular on the many islands of western Scotland.

Norse

This was the language brought by the Viking invaders of the eighth century, or perhaps even earlier, and has left a sizeable impression on the place-names of the Western Isles and the west coast, where the jagged coastline pro-

Iona Cathedral stands on the site of St Columba's monastery

vided ideal harbours and settling-places for the Norsemen.

English

English may have been spoken in the area between Berwick-on-Tweed and Edinburgh as early as the fifth century, but did not spread to the rest of Scotland until around the eleventh century, and indeed, did not make much impression on the speech of most of the Highlands until the 1745 Rebellion. It has, of course, ousted the others almost entirely since then. Naturally enough, English place-names are more common in southern Scotland than in the north. Lowland Scottish is a variation of English.

Latin and French

Latin and its descendant, French, have only made a slight impression on Scottish place-names. There are a few French names such as Melville (*mal ville*) and Belses (from de Bel Assize, a personal name) which are probably Norman. Other French-influenced names, such as Burdiehouse, are thought to be the result of the 'Auld Alliance' between France and Scotland. The minor influence of Latin owes more to the church than to the Roman occupation, which was limited in its extent or success, in Scotland. One important Latin word in Scottish place-names is *ecclesia* – 'church', which is the root of the Gaelic for church, *eaglis*, and of names containing 'Eccles-' or 'Eglis-', such as Ecclefechan – 'church of St Fiachan'.

The broad outline of the linguistic features of Scotland's place-names is as follows, English/Scottish (Birnam,

Bishopton); Latin/French (Ecclefechan, Burdiehouse);
Norse (Wick, Kirkwall); Gaelic or Q-Celtic (Balloch,
Ardmore); Brittonic or P-Celtic (Pitlochry, Aberdeen);
Pre-Celtic (River Names: Tay, Nairn, Ayr etc.). It should
be borne in mind that there is a considerable overlap
between these language groups. For instance, Norse *gardr*,
an enclosure, appears in Brittonic as *garth*, Gaelic as *garradh* and English as garden. Norse *vik*, a bay, was adopted
in Gaelic as the common suffix *-aig* with the same meaning. The Pictish Brittonic word *pett* meaning a piece,
share, is present in names such as Pittenweem, Pitcaple
and Pitlochry, but is usually found in conjunction with
Gaelic second elements. In the case of Pitlochry, the second element is *cloichreach* – 'stony'. These names cannot
really be classified as Brittonic or Pictish on the basis of
the *pett* element alone, although the 300 or so of these
names in the north-east of Scotland provide strong evidence of the presence of Pictish Brittonic speaking
inhabitants in this area. The *pett* element was obviously
adopted into Gaelic as a name for these old-established,
well-situated and, according to geographical evidence,
probably flourishing communities. Having been adopted,
it became part of Gaelic, although not used except in
relation to place-names. It is cognate with Welsh *peth* – 'a
thing', Breton *pez* – 'piece', ancient Gaullish *petia*, from
which comes French *piece* and its Gaelic descendant is *cuid*,
a portion.

Language divisions are not sharp and places may have
names in several languages. Many have names in Gaelic
as well as English. Pitlochry is known in Gaelic as
Bailechlochry. The town of Falkirk has had names in three
languages as well as English; *eaglis breac* in Gaelic, *La Vaire
Chapelle* in French and *Varia Capella* in Latin, all of which
mean 'speckled church', perhaps a reference to the type of
stone of which the church was built. This is a particularly

well-documented name, and emphasises the importance of knowing old spellings, and, hence, old pronunciations, since the Old English *faw,* meaning speckled, has been obscured by the modern 'Fal-' spelling, although its meaning is quite clear when the old forms and translations are seen. The local pronunciation is, in fact, still 'Fawkirk'.

Modern spellings can be very deceptive indeed. The Borders village of Oxton would appear at first glance to be a straightforward English name meaning town of the oxen. But evidence that its name at around 1200 was Ulfkilston, indicates that a contraction has taken place, to the point where the Old English personal name, Ulfkil, is no longer recognisable. The name of the village has nothing whatsoever to do with oxen.

Spelling mistakes have even played their part in the development of some names; Iona is thought by some to be a scribe's mis-spelling of the original name, Ioua, and Findochty in Grampian is the result of a mis-spelling of 'Findechty' on the sign at the railway station, when the railway was constructed in the nineteenth century. The new name, perhaps considered more 'correct' stuck, although locals still call it 'Finechty'.

It is important, then, in the study of place-names, to have details of old names and pronunciations, but this need not deter those whose interest is more casual from trying to decipher the meaning of names for themselves, for in many cases in Scotland there are recurrent words, mainly Gaelic, which give clues to a name's meaning.

BEYOND PLACE-NAMES

Most of this book, and the introduction so far, is concerned with the etymology of place-names; their historical and linguistic past and the meanings which are hidden in them. Some place-names, however, do not stop there. They have a future as well, and carry on to be used in other areas of language.

Surnames

The practice of using place-names to distinguish people of the same surname was widespread in Scotland, because there was often a concentration of two or three surnames in each village, and by-names had to be invented to prevent confusion. The obvious way of distinguishing farmers, for instance, was by using the name of their farm, e.g. Tam of Todshaws. This practice led to some place-names becoming surnames, such as Leslie, Lennox, Ogilvie and Urquhart. Similarly, landowners were known as a matter of courtesy, by their territorial name; Cameron of Lochiel, for instance. James Boswell, remarks in his *Jour-*

James Boswell with Dr Johnson in the Hebrides

13

nal of a tour to the Hebrides that the laird was addressed simply by the name of his territory, and that it was 'somewhat droll' to hear the laird of the island of Muck being addressed by his title, 'Muck'.

Social meaning

There is another aspect to meaning in place-names, and that is the social or historical connotation which a name may carry. Most people in Britain, for example, at the mention of the name Barlinnie, would think of a prison, not a hill with a pool, its etymological meaning. Culloden brings to mind a great battle, and Loch Ness the world-famous monster. Most place-names, in fact, carry connotations of this kind, sometimes known only to local people and sometimes known more widely. Kelvinside in Glasgow, for instance, was known throughout Scotland as an area where well-off citizens with some social pretensions chose to live, and although the area itself is no longer particularly wealthy or snobbish, the notion of a 'Kelvinside accent' lingers on. At the other extreme in Glasgow, the Gorbals developed a notoriety as a very rough area.

Music and Literature

In Aberdeen, a local music-hall comedian of the thirties, called Harry Gordon, encapsulated the connotations of some local names in one of his songs, which begins:

> Fitty folk, Kitty folk
> Country folk and city folk,
> Folk fae Constitution Street,
> And folk fae Rubislaw Den, . . .

Fitty and Kittybrewster being geographically distant from one another, while Constitution Street and Rubislaw Den are at opposing ends of the social spectrum. Billy Connolly does little for the image of the Clydeside resort of Saltcoats in his song *Saltcoats at the Fair*, while, to go from the ridiculous to the sublime, Mendelssohn did wonders for that of the Hebrides through his music. Robert Burns's poems, and in particular, Sir Walter Scott's novels set in Scotland, have immortalised various Scottish place-names.

There are, in fact, innumerable Scottish songs which mention place-names, *Loch Lomond* being one of the most famous. Many of these songs deal with the nostalgic longing of Scottish exiles to return to their birthplace: *Take me home to Ardentinny, Westering Home to Islay, By Tummel and Loch Rannoch and Lochaber I will go . . ., Gin I where Gadie rins*. The list is endless.

Exports

Besides whisky, one of Scotland's greatest exports has been its people. Sentimental longing for the home country is seen in the songs mentioned above, and in the numerous Scottish place-names to be found throughout the ex-colonies. Perth, in Australia, Dunedin, the Gaelic name for Edinburgh, in New Zealand, Banff, Calgary and numerous others in North America and even Aberdeen in Hong Kong, are names given by Scottish immigrants. In North America, this results in an interesting re-arrangement of Scotland's geography, and some of the new settlements are, ironically, much larger than the towns or villages they are named after. Many of the Scottish place-names found in America are directly from personal or territorial names, not the place-names themselves. Athol in Massachusetts is from the Duke of Atholl, Albany from the Duke of York and Albany, Elgin Oregon from a lake steamer called the Lady Elgin and Stirling from a self-styled Lord Stirling. Others are from literature – Midlothian in Texas and various Montroses are drawn from the writings of Sir Walter Scott.

Besides these specific areas into which Scottish place-names have been extended, there are numerous examples of names becoming used to describe other things – Clydesdale horse, Ayrshire cattle, Paisley shawls, Crombie coats, Fair Isle sweaters, and so on. One interesting and rather surprising example is the mineral strontium, which was named after Strontian (Highland) because it was first discovered there in the eighteenth century.

COMMON ELEMENTS IN SCOTTISH PLACE-NAMES

aber	Brittonic	confluence, river mouth
ach, auch	Gaelic	field
alt, auld, ault	Gaelic	stream
ard	Gaelic	promontory
auchter	Gaelic	top, high place
bal	Gaelic	farm, village
barr	Gaelic	top, summit
balloch	Gaelic	pass
ben	Gaelic	hill
blair	Gaelic	pass
bost	Norse	farm, village
brae	Gaelic	slope
by	Norse	farm, village
cairn	Gaelic	cairn, heap of stones
corry	Gaelic	corry, hollow
craig	Gaelic	crag, hill
dal	Gaelic	field, valley

drum	Gaelic	back, ridge
dun, dum	Gaelic	fortress, hill
eccles, eglis	Gaelic	church
ey, ay, a	Norse	island
fetter	Gaelic	slope
four	Brittonic	pasture
gart, garth	Norse	garden, yard
glen	Gaelic	valley
inch, innis	Gaelic	island
inver	Gaelic	confluence, mouth
kil	Gaelic	church
kin	Gaelic	head, at the head
kirk	Scottish	church
kyle	Gaelic	strait, narrow
letter	Gaelic	slope, hillside
lin, linn	Gaelic	lake, pool
loch	Gaelic	lake
more	Gaelic	big
ness	Norse	promontory
ochter	Gaelic	upper part
pit	Brittonic	share, portion
pol, pool	Gaelic	pool
ros, ross	Gaelic	promontory
strath	Gaelic	valley
strone	Gaelic	nose, point
torr, tra	Gaelic	hill, castle
tilly, tulloch	Gaelic	hill
voe, way, wall	Norse	bay
vik, wick	Norse	bay

SCOTTISH PLACE-NAMES

ABERCHIRDER (Grampian) 'Mouth of the dark stream';
Brittonic *aber* – 'mouth', Gaelic *chiar* – 'dark' and *dobhar* –
'water, stream'. Known locally as 'Fogie Loan', which is
obscure in its meaning.

ABERCROMBIE (Fife) Now called St Monans. 'Crooked
river-mouth'; Brittonic *aber* – 'confluence, mouth' and Gaelic
crom – 'crooked'.

ABERDEEN (Grampian) 'At the mouth of the River Don';
Brittonic *aber* – 'mouth' and Gaelic *Deathan* – Don. Old
Aberdeen is at the mouth of the River Don, not the River
Dee, although the Dee has probably influenced the modern
spelling.

ABERDOUR (Fife) 'At the mouth of the River Dour'; Brittonic
aber – 'mouth' and Gaelic *dobhar* – 'water, stream'.

ABERFELDY (Tayside) 'River-mouth of Paldoc'; Brittonic
aber – 'mouth'. Paldoc was a disciple of St Ninian.

ABERFOYLE (Central) 'Pool-mouth'; Brittonic *aber* – 'mouth'
and Gaelic *phuill* – 'pool'.

ABERLEMNO (Tayside) 'Mouth of the elm-stream'; Brittonic
aber – 'mouth' and Gaelic *leamhan* – 'elm'.

ABOYNE (Grampian) 'Foaming river'; Gaelic *abh* – 'river' and
omhan – 'foam'.

ACHANALT (Highland) 'Field by the burn'; Gaelic *achadh* – 'field' and *allt* – 'burn, stream'.

ACHILTIBUIE (Highland) 'Field of the yellow-haired lad'; Gaelic *achadh* – 'field', *ghille* – 'lad' and *buidhe* – 'yellow-haired'.

ACHLUACHRACH (Highland) 'Rushy field'; Gaelic *achadh* – 'field' and *luachair* – 'rushes'.

ACHNACARRY (Highland) 'Field of the weir'; Gaelic *achadh* – 'field' and *caraidh* – 'weir' or 'fish-trap'.

ACHNACLOICH (Highland) 'Field of the stone'; Gaelic *achadh* – 'field' and *clach* – 'stone'.

ACHNAHANAT (Highland) 'Field of the patron saint's church'; Gaelic *achadh* – 'field' and *annaid* – 'mother-church' or church of a patron saint.

ACHNASHEEN (Highland) 'Field of storms'; Gaelic *achadh* – 'field' and *sian* – 'storm'.

ACHNASHELLACH (Highland) 'Field of willows'; Gaelic *achadh* – 'field' and *seilach* – 'willow'.

ACKERGILL (Highland) 'Untilled ravine'; Norse *akr* – 'untilled land' and *gil* – 'ravine'.

AFFLECK (Grampian and Tayside) 'Stony field'; Gaelic *achadh* – 'field' and *leac* – 'flat stone, slab'.

AIRDRIE (Strathclyde) 'High hill-pasture'; Gaelic *aird* – 'high' and *airidh* – 'hill pasture', or perhaps *ruighe* – 'slope'.

ALEXANDRIA (Strathclyde) Named after Alexander Smollet, MP for Bonhill, 1760.

ALLOA (Central) 'Rocky place'; Gaelic *ailbheach*. ALVA (Central) and ALYTH (Tayside) are also derived from this word, based on *ail* – 'a rock', and have the same meaning.

ALNESS (Highland) Probably from the River Alness, which is a pre-Celtic river name thought to mean 'holy' or 'mighty' river. Also a connection with Gaelic *ailean* – 'meadow'.

ALTNABREAC (Highland) 'Stream of the trout'; Gaelic *allt* – 'stream' and *breac* – 'trout'.

ANCRUM (Borders) 'Bend of the River Alne'; Gaelic *cromadh* – 'bend'.

ANGUS (Tayside) 'Territory of Angus' son of Fergus, eighth century king of the Picts.

ANSTRUTHER (Fife) 'The little stream'; Gaelic *an* – 'the' and *sruthair* – 'little stream'. Could also be from Old English *engi struther* – 'marshy meadow'.

APPLECROSS (Highland) 'Mouth of the River Crossan'; Brittonic *aber* – 'mouth'. *Crossain* means 'little cross' in Gaelic. The river is now called the Applecross, after the village.

ARBIRLOT (Tayside) 'Ford on Elliot Water'; Gaelic *ath* – 'ford'.

ARBROATH (Tayside) Formerly 'Aberbrothock' – 'mouth of the Brothock burn'; Brittonic *aber* – 'mouth', and Gaelic *brothach* – 'seething river'.

ARDALANISH (Strathclyde) Gaelic *ard gheal* – 'white cape' and Norse *nes* – 'cape'.

ARDCHATTAN (Strathclyde) 'Height of Abbot Chattan'; Gaelic *ard*. St Chattan was a contemporary of St Columba, third century.

ARDEER (Strathclyde) 'Westcape'; Gaelic *ard* – 'cape' and *iar* – 'west'.

ARDENTINNY (Strathclyde) 'Height of the fire'; Gaelic *ard* – 'height' and *teine* – 'fire'. Fire was a signal for the ferryman here.

ARDERSIER (Highland) 'High east point'; Gaelic *ard* – 'high', *ros* – 'point' and *ear* – 'east'.

ARDGOUR (Highland) 'Promontory of Gabran'; Gaelic *ard* – 'height, promontory' and the personal name. Or possibly 'promontory of the goat' from Gaelic *gobhar* – 'goat'.

ARDMORE (Highland) 'Big promontory'; Gaelic *ard* – 'promontory' and *mor* – 'big'.

ARDNAMURCHAN (Highland) 'Height of the otter'; Gaelic *ard* – 'height' and *muirchu* – 'otter'.

Ardnamurchan

ARDOCH (Tayside) 'High place'; Gaelic *ard* – 'high'.

ARDRISHAIG (Strathclyde) 'Height of the brambles'; Gaelic *ard* – 'height' and *dris* – 'bramble'.

ARDROSS (Highland) 'High headland'; Gaelic *ard* – 'high' and *ros* – 'headland'. ARDROSSAN (Strathclyde) is 'height of the little cape' from the same Gaelic derivation with the diminutive *-an*.

ARDTORNISH POINT (Highland) The notion of a point is repeated three times in this name. It means 'promontory of the point of Thori', from Gaelic *ard* – 'promontory', the Norse name *Thori* and Gaelic *nish* – 'point', plus 'point' in English.

ARGYLL (Highland) 'Land of the Gaels'; Gaelic *earr* – 'boundary, land' and *a' Ghaideal* – 'of the Gaels'.

ARROCHAR (Strathclyde) From 'carrucate', a measure of land equivalent to a ploughgate, which owes its linguistic origin to the Latin for a ploughgate, *aratrum*. See OXGANGS (Lothian).

ARRAN (Strathclyde) Brittonic *aran* – 'peaked hill'.

ARTHUR'S SEAT (Lothian) Said to be named after the famous sixth-century king, Arthur.

ATHELSTANEFORD (Lothian) Where Athelstone, a Northumbrian general, was defeated by a Pictish king c750.

21

AUCHENCAIRN (Dumfries & Galloway) 'Field with the cairn'; Gaelic *achadh* – 'field', *an cairn*. AUCHINAIRN (Strathclyde) has the same meaning and derivation.

AUCHENDINNY (Lothian) 'Field of refuge'; Gaelic *achadh* – 'field' and *dion* – 'refuge'.

AUCHENHEATH (Strathclyde) 'Field of birch'; Gaelic *achadh* – 'field' and *beithe* – 'birch'.

AUCHINLECK (Strathclyde) 'Field of the flat stone'; Gaelic *achadh* – 'field' and *leac* – 'flat stone'.

AUCHMORE (Strathclyde, Arran) 'Big field'; Gaelic *achadh* – 'field' and *mor* – 'big'. This is the old name: the village is now called THUNDERGAY.

AUCHTERARDER (Tayside) 'Upland of the high water'; Gaelic *uachdar* – 'upland', *ard* – 'high' and *dobhar* – 'water'.

AUCHTERHOUSE (Tayside) 'Field of the ghost'; Gaelic *achadh* – 'field' and *fhuathais* – 'ghost, spectre'. AULD-HOUSE (Strathclyde) is a similar corruption of *fhuathais*.

AUCHTERLESS (Grampian) 'Upland with the garden'; Gaelic *uachdar* and *lios* – 'garden'.

AUCHTERMUCHTY (Fife) 'Upland of the pigs'; Gaelic *uachdar* and *muice* – 'pig'.

AULTBEA (Highland) 'Birch burn'; Gaelic *allt* – 'stream, burn' and *beithe* – 'birch'.

AVIEMORE (Highland) 'Big hill-face'; Gaelic *aghaidh* – 'hill-face' and *mor* – 'big'.

AVOCH (Highland) 'River-place'; Gaelic *abhainn* – 'river'.

AYR (Strathclyde) From the River Ayr. Old pre-Celtic river name.

BADENOCH (Highland) 'Marshy land'; Gaelic *baidheanach*.

BALDOVAN (Tayside) 'Poor hamlet'; Gaelic *baile* – 'village' and *doimh* – 'poor'.

BALERNO (Lothian) 'Barley farm'; Gaelic *baile* – 'village' and *eorna* – 'barley'.

BALFOUR (Tayside) 'Village on the pasture land'; Gaelic *baile* – 'village' and Brittonic *pawr* – 'pasture land'. PITFOUR (Tayside) has a similar meaning.

BALGONIE (Fife) 'Village of the smiths'; Gaelic *baile* – 'village' and *gobhainn* – 'smiths'. BALGOWAN (Highland) and BALGOWNIE (Grampian) have the same, or similar, meaning and derivation.

BALLACHULISH (Highland) 'Village on the straits'; Gaelic *baile* – 'village' and *caolas* – 'strait, kyle'.

BALLANTRAE (Strathclyde) 'Village on the shore'; Gaelic *baile* – 'village' and *traigh* – 'beach'.

BALLATER (Grampian) 'Pass-land'; Gaelic *bealach* – 'pass' and *tir* – 'land'.

BALLINDALLOCH (Grampian) 'Village in the field'; Gaelic *baile* – 'village' and *dalach* – 'of the field'.

BALLINTUIM (Tayside) 'Village on the hillock'; Gaelic *baile* – 'village' and *tuim* – 'hillock', or sometimes 'copse'.

BALLOCH (Strathclyde & Highland) 'A pass'; Gaelic *bealach* – 'pass'. BEALACH NAM BO (Central) is the 'pass for the cattle'.

BALLOCHMYLE (Strathclyde) 'Bare pass'; Gaelic *bealach* – 'pass' and *maol* – 'bare'.

BALMAHA (Central) 'St Maha's village'; Gaelic *baile* – 'village'. St Maha's well is nearby.

BALMORAL (Grampian) 'Village in the big clearing'; Gaelic *baile* – 'village, *mor* – 'big' and Brittonic *ial* – 'clearing'. This is an example of the Brittonic *Pit* being superseded by Gaelic *Baile*. Its modern Gaelic name is *Baile mhoireir* – 'laird's dwelling' and a perhaps more appropriate, if rather fanciful, interpretation of the name is 'majestic village' from Gaelic *moral* – 'majestic', as the sovereign has a residence here.

BALNAGUARD (Tayside) 'Village of the craftsman'; Gaelic *baile* – 'village' and *ceard* – 'craftsman, smith'.

23

BALQUHIDDER (Central) 'Fodder farm'; Gaelic *baile* – 'farm, village' and *fuidir* – 'fodder'.

BANAVIE (Highland) 'Place of pigs'; Irish *banbh* – 'sucking pig'.

BANCHORY (Grampian) 'Place of peaks'; Gaelic *beannachar*. 'Banchory-Devenick' and 'Banchory-Ternan' refer to Saints Devenick and Ternan.

BANFF (Grampian) 'Land unploughed for one year'; Gaelic *banbh*, which also means 'sucking pig'.

BANNOCKBURN (Central) 'White stream'; Brittonic *ban oc* – 'white stream' and Scottish *burn*.

BARCALDINE (Strathclyde) 'Hazel height'; Gaelic *barr* – 'top, height' and *calltuinn* – 'hazel'.

BARDOWIE (Strathclyde) 'Dark height'; Gaelic *barr* – 'top, summit' and *dubh* – 'dark'.

BARLINNIE (Strathclyde) 'Height with the pool'; Gaelic *barr* – 'height' and *linne* – 'pool'.

BARRHEAD (Strathclyde) 'Top head'; Gaelic *barr* – 'top' and English *head*. Tautology.

BATHGATE (Lothian) Brittonic *both* – 'house' and *chet* – 'in the wood', or perhaps 'boar wood'; Brittonic *baedd*.

BAYBLE (Western Isles, Lewis) Corruption of Norse *papa-bol* – 'priest's dwelling'.

BEATH (Fife) 'A birch'; Gaelic *beath*.

BEAULY (Highland) 'Lovely place'; French *beau lieu*.

BEESWING (Dumfries & Galloway) Named after a picture of a racehorse, called Beeswing, used as a pub-sign. The village grew around the pub.

BEITH (Strathclyde) 'A birch'; Gaelic *beath*.

BELHELVIE (Grampian) 'Village of Sealbhach'; Gaelic *baile* – 'village'.

BELLAHOUSTON (Strathclyde) 'Village with the crucifix'; Gaelic *baile a' cheusadain*. The present form indicates identification in the popular mind with a non-existent woman, called 'Bella Houston'. (See KITTYBREWSTER).

24

BELLOCHANTUY (Strathclyde) 'Pass of the seat'; Gaelic *bealach* – 'pass', *an suidhe* – 'of the seat'.

BENBECULA (Western Isles) Perhaps 'hill of the fords'; Gaelic *beinn* – 'hill', *na fhaodha* – 'of the fords'.

BENDERLOCH (Strathclyde) 'Hill between lochs'; Gaelic *beinn* – 'hill' and *eadar* – 'between'.

BENTPATH (Dumfries & Galloway) Path through *bennet* or reed-like grass.

BERWICK, NORTH (Lothian) 'Outlying farm'; Old English *bere* – 'barley' and *wic* – 'dwelling'.

BETTYHILL (Highland) Named after Elizabeth, Countess of Sutherland c1820. Built to re-house those evicted during Highland Clearances.

BIGGAR (Strathclyde) 'Barley field'; Norse *bygg* – 'barley' and *gardr* – 'field'.

BIRGHAM (Borders) 'Village at the bridge'; Old English *bricg* – 'bridge' and *ham* – 'village'.

BIRNAM (Tayside) 'Warrior's home'; Old English *biorn* – 'warrior' and *ham* – 'home, village'.

BIRRENSWARK (Dumfries & Galloway) 'Bruna's fort'; Old English *weorc* – 'fortification'.

BISHOPBRIGGS (Strathclyde) Bridge of the Bishop of Glasgow.

BIXTER (Shetland) 'Barley farm'; Norse *bygg* – 'barley' and *setr* – 'farm, house'.

BLADNOCH (Dumfries & Galloway) 'Place of splinters'; Gaelic *bloideanach*.

BLAIRGOWRIE (Tayside) 'Plain of Gowrie'; Gaelic *blar* – 'plain' and the territory of Gabran, a figure in Celtic legend.

BLAIRLOGIE (Central) 'Plain in a hollow'; Gaelic *blar* – 'plain' and *luig* – 'hollow'.

BLAIRMORE (Highland and Strathclyde) 'Big plain'; Gaelic *blar mhor*.

25

Blantyre

BLANTYRE (Strathclyde) 'Edge, end-land'; Brittonic *blaentir*.

BOAT OF GARTEN (Highland) Ferry of Garten, Gaelic *gairtean* – 'croft'.

BODDAM (Grampian and Shetland) Scottish for 'valley bottom'.

BOISDALE, NORTH (Western Isles, S. Uist) 'Bay valley'; Norse *bugis* – 'bay' and *dalr* – 'valley'.

BOLTON (Lothian) Old English *botl-tun* – 'enclosure of dwellings, village'.

BONALY (Lothian) 'House on the rock'; Gaelic *both* – 'house' and *na h'aile* – 'on the rock'.

BO'NESS (Central) Originally 'Borrowstounness'. *Borrowstoune*; Scottish for municipal burgh, from Norse *borg* – 'fort', and Norse *nes* – 'headland'. The town was once closer to sea than it now is.

BONHILL (Strathclyde) 'House by the stream'; Gaelic *both* – 'house' and *an uidh* – 'by the stream'.

BONNINGTON (Lothian) 'Village of Bond, the bondsman or householder'.

BORELAND (Dumfries & Galloway) Old Norse *bord* – 'table' and 'land'. There was a home farm here which supplied the lord's table.

26

BORGUE (Dumfries & Galloway and Highland) 'Fort, stronghold'; Norse *borg* – 'fort'. (See BORVE, BROUGH).

BORNISH (Western Isles, S. Uist) 'Fort headland'; Norse *borg* – 'fort' and *nes* – 'headland', in Gaelic – *nish*.

BORVE (Western Isles, several) 'Fort'; Norse *borg*. (See BORGUE, BROUGH).

BOTHWELL (Strathclyde) 'Hut by the pool'; Old English *bothe* – 'hut' and *woel* – 'by the pool'.

BOWLING (Strathclyde) 'Place of the sons of Bolla'. Old English.

BOWMORE (Strathclyde) 'Big house'; Gaelic *both* – 'house' and *mor* – 'big'.

BRACADALE (Highland, Skye) 'Valley with the steep slope'; Norse *brekka* – 'slope' and *dalr* – 'valley'.

BRACO (Tayside) 'Grey place'; Gaelic *bracach*.

BRAEMAR (Grampian) 'Upper part' of Mar; Gaelic *braighe*. 'Mar' seems to have been a tribal or family name in the area.

BRAID (Lothian) 'Upper part'; Gaelic *braghad*.

BRAIDWOOD (Strathclyde) 'Broad wood'; Scottish *braid* – 'broad'.

BRANXHOLME (Borders) 'Meadow of Brance'. Norse *holm* – 'island' or 'meadow'.

BREADALBANE (Central) Gaelic *braghad Albainn* – 'upper part of Alban'.

BRECHIN (Tayside) Place of Brychan, a Brittonic personal name. He is thought to have been the founder of Brechin.

BRIDGE OF ALLAN (Central) Bridge over Allan Water, from Gaelic *alainn* – 'beautiful'.

BRIDGE OF CALLY (Tayside) From Gaelic *caladh* – 'ferry, harbour'.

BRODICK (Strathclyde, Arran) 'Broad bay'; Norse *breid vik*.

BRORA (Highland) 'Bridge river'; Norse *bru* – 'bridge' and *a* – 'river'. This was once the only bridge in Sutherland.

27

BROUGH (Shetland) Norse *borg* – 'fort'.

BRUICHLADDICH (Strathclyde) 'Bank on the shore'; Gaelic *bruach* – 'bank' and *chladaich* – 'on the shore'.

BUCCLEUCH (Borders) 'Buck's glen'; Norse *bukk* – 'a buck' and Scottish *cleugh* – 'glen, gorge'.

BUCHAN (Grampian) Very old, perhaps pre-Celtic. Or may be from Gaelic *baogh* – 'a calf', 'calf-place'. The BULLERS OF BUCHAN (Grampian) which so impressed Dr Johnson, are huge circular caverns, like cauldrons, which the water enters from below, seeming almost to boil in stormy weather, thus giving them their name 'boilers' or 'bullers'.

BUCHANAN (Central) 'House of the canon'; Gaelic *both* – 'house' and *chanain* – 'of the canon'.

BUCHLYVIE (Central) 'House on the hill'; Gaelic *both* – 'house' and *sleibhe* – 'on the hill'.

BUCKIE (Grampian) 'Pimple, knob'; Gaelic *bucaidh*.

BUNCHREW (Highland) 'At the foot of the trees'; Gaelic *bun* – 'near, at the foot of' and *chraoibhe* – 'trees'.

BURDIEHOUSE (Lothian) Said to be 'Bordeaux house', because of French settlers, or perhaps Mary Queen of Scots' French attendants.

BURGHEAD (Grampian) Site of *borg* – 'fort', built by Norsemen c880.

BURNTISLAND (Fife) Said to be because of fishers' huts burnt on islet near harbour. May also be 'Burnet's island'.

CAIRNBAAN (Strathclyde) 'White cairn'; Gaelic *ban* – 'white'.

CAIRNGORM (Grampian/Highland) 'Greenish blue cairn, hill'; Gaelic *gorm* – 'green-blue'.

CAIRNRYAN (Dumfries & Galloway) So named in nineteenth century. Formerly 'Macharyskeeg'; Gaelic *machar a' sgitheach* – 'plain of hawthorn'.

CAITHNESS (Highland) 'Promontory of the Cats', the tribal name of the early Celtic people who lived here; Norse *nes* – 'promontory'. In Gaelic called *Gallaibh* – 'land of strangers', perhaps the Norsemen.

CALDER, EAST & WEST (Highland and Lothian) 'Hazel stream'; Gaelic *call* – 'stream' and *dobhar* – 'water'.

CALDERCRUIX (Strathclyde) 'Crooks, windings of the River Calder'.

CALEDONIA Latinised name for Scotland, named after the Caledones, a tribe who inhabited an area of Central Scotland; Brittonic *caled* – 'hard', so 'the hard people'.

CALIFORNIA (Central) Transferred from the United States.

CALLANDER (Central) 'Hazel stream'; Gaelic *call* – 'hazel' and *dobhar* – 'water'. CALLATER (Grampian) and CALDER (Highland and Lothian) have the same meaning and derivation.

CALTON (Strathclyde and Lothian) 'Hazel'; Gaelic *caltuinn*.

CAMBUS (Central) 'Bay, creek'; Gaelic *camas* – 'bay, bend, creek'.

CAMBUSBARRON (Central) 'Bend at the little height'; Gaelic *camas* – 'bend' and *barran* – 'little top, hill, height'.

CAMBUSLANG (Strathclyde) 'Creek of the ship'; Gaelic *camas* – 'creek' and *long* – 'ship', recently confused with Scottish *lang*.

CAMPBELTOWN (Strathclyde) Named 1598 after Earl of Argyll, head of Clan Campbell.

CAMUSNAGAUL (Highland) 'Creek of the stranger'; Gaelic *camas* – 'creek' and *gall* – 'stranger'.

CANNA (Highland) 'Island like a can, or pot'; Norse *kanna* – 'can' and *ey* – 'island'.

CANONBIE (Dumfries & Galloway) 'Village of the canon'. Priory founded here 1165. Norse *byr* – 'village'.

CAOL (Highland) 'Kyle, strait'; Gaelic *caol*.   29

CARBERRY (Lothian) 'Wooded height'; Gaelic *craobh* – 'tree' and *barr* – 'height, top'.

CARDENDEN (Fife) 'Valley of the thicket'; Brittonic *cardden* – 'thicket' and 'den', English.

CARDONALD (Strathclyde) 'Fort of Donald'; Gaelic *cathair* – 'fort'.

CARDROSS (Strathclyde) 'Rowan tree promontory'; Brittonic *cerdin rhos*.

CARMYLE (Strathclyde) 'Bare rock'; Gaelic *carn* – 'rock' and *maol* – 'bare'.

CARNOCH (Highland) 'Rocky place'; Gaelic *carnach*.

CARNOUSTIE (Tayside) 'Rock of the firtree'; Gaelic *carn na giuthas*.

CARRICK (Strathclyde) 'Rock'; Gaelic *carraig* – 'rock'.

CARRIDEN (Central) 'Fort on the slope'; Brittonic *caer* – 'fort' and *eiddyn* – 'on the slope'.

CARRINGTON (Lothian) 'Village of the descendants of *Carr*'. Old English.

CASTLECARY (Central) Repetition of 'castle'; Brittonic *caer* – 'castle, fort' and English.

CASTLE DOUGLAS (Dumfries & Galloway) Originally 'Carlinwark'. Re-named 1792 after Sir William Douglas.

CATACOL (Strathclyde) 'Ravine of the wild cats'; Norse *gil* – 'ravine' and *katta* – 'cat'.

CATHKIN (Strathclyde) 'Upland of the battle'; Gaelic *cath* – 'battle' and *cinn* – 'head, headland'.

CATTERLINE (Grampian) 'Fort of the pool'; Gaelic *cathair* – 'fort' and *linne* – 'pool'.

CAUSEWAYEND (Central) End of causeway from Stirling Castle to Stirling Bridge.

CAWDOR (Highland) 'Hazel stream'; Gaelic *call* – 'hazel' and *dobhar* – 'water'.

CLACHAN (Strathclyde and Highland, Skye) Gaelic for 'place of stones, house or village'; *clach* – 'stone'.

Clydebank

CLACHNAHARRY (Highland) 'Stone of watching'; Gaelic *clach* – 'stone' and *na fhaire* – 'of watching'.

CLACKMANNAN (Central) 'Stone of Manu'; reference to a stone in the middle of the village.

CLARKSTON (Strathclyde) 'Village of the cleric or clerk'.

CLETT (Highland and Skye) 'Cliff'; Gaelic *cleit*.

CLAUCHLANDS (Strathclyde) 'Rocky land'; Gaelic *clach* – 'rock'.

CLEISH (Tayside) 'A ditch'; Gaelic *clais*.

CLOSEBURN (Dumfries & Galloway) 'Church of St Osborne'; Gaelic *cill Osbern*.

CLYDEBANK (Strathclyde) On the banks of the River Clyde. 'Clyde' may be related to Brittonic *clyd* – 'warm'.

COATBRIDGE (Strathclyde) Bridge built c1800. Brittonic *coed* – 'a wood' or perhaps referring to the cot-town (cottage-town) where the bridge was built.

COCKPEN (Lothian) 'Red head'; Brittonic *coch* – 'red' and *pen* – 'head, edge'.

COLDSTREAM (Borders) Perhaps referring to the River Tweed.

COLINTRAIVE (Strathclyde) 'The swimming strait'; Gaelic *caol* – 'strait' and *snaimh* – 'of swimming'. Drovers used to cross over from Bute with their cattle here.

COLLIESTON (Grampian) 'Town of Collie'; Old English *tun*. Collie is a common local personal name.

COLONSAY (Strathclyde) 'St Columba's island'; Colum's *ey*; Norse – 'island'.

COMRIE (Fife and Tayside) 'Confluence'; Gaelic *comar* and *ie* suffix of place.

CORPACH (Highland) 'Corpse-place'; where corpses used to be kept overnight, when travelling to a burial isle.

CORRAN (Highland) 'Pointed headland'; Gaelic *corran* – 'sickle, beak, headland'.

CORRIEVRECKAN (Strathclyde) 'Whirlpool, cauldron of Brecon'; Gaelic *coire* – 'corrie, cauldron' and the name *Bhrecain*.

CORSTORPHINE (Lothian) 'Cross of Thorfinn', Earl of the Orkneys, eleventh century.

COULTER (Strathclyde) and CULTER (Grampian) 'Back land'; Gaelic *cul* – 'back' and *tir* – 'land'.

COWDENBEATH (Fife) 'Birch at the back of the hill'; Gaelic *cul* – 'back', *duin* – 'of the hill' and *beithe* – 'birch'.

CRAIGELLACHIE (Grampian) 'Rocky crag'; Gaelic *creag* – 'crag' and *eileach* – 'rocky'.

CRAIGMILLAR (Lothian) 'Rock of the bare height'; Gaelic *creag, maol* – 'bare' and *ard* – 'height'.

CRAIL (Fife) 'Rocky cliff'; Gaelic *carraig* – 'rock' and *ail* – 'rock'. Tautology.

CRAMOND (Lothian) 'Fort on the River Almond'; Brittonic *caer* – 'fort'.

CRIEFF (Tayside) 'Among the trees'; Gaelic *craobh* – 'tree'.

CROMARTY (Highland) 'Crooked height'; Gaelic *crom* – 'crooked' and ard — 'height'.

CROOKSTON (Strathclyde) Named after Robert de Croc, a Norman nobleman, in the twelfth century.

CROSSMYLOOF (Strathclyde) 'Cross of Malduff'; Gaelic *crois* – 'cross'.

CRUDEN BAY (Grampian) 'Kingfisher bay'; Gaelic *cruidein.*

CULLEN (Grampian) 'Little nook'; Gaelic *cuilan.*

CULLODEN (Highland) 'The back of the little pool'; Gaelic *cul* – 'back' and *lodain* – 'little pool'.

CULROSS (Highland) 'Holly wood'; Gaelic *cuileann* – 'holly' and *ros* – 'wood'.

CUMBERNAULD (Strathclyde) 'Meeting of the streams'; Gaelic *comar* – 'confluence' and *an allt* – 'of the streams'.

CUMBRAE (LITTLE and GREAT) (Strathclyde) 'Isles of the Cymri' or Welsh.

CUMNOCK, NEW (Strathclyde) 'Little strait'; Gaelic *cumhann* – 'strait'.

CUPAR (Fife) 'Common land'; Gaelic *comhpairt.*

DALBEATTIE (Dumfries & Galloway) 'Field of the birch trees'; Gaelic *dail* – 'field' and *beithe* – 'birch'.

DALKEITH (Lothian) 'Field in the wood'; Brittonic *dol* – 'field, meadow' and *coed* – 'tree, wood'.

DALMALLY (Strathclyde) 'Field of mail'; Gaelic *dail* – 'field' and *mhailidh* – 'mail, armour'.

DALMARNOCK (Strathclyde) 'Field of St Mernoc'; Gaelic *dail* – 'field, dale'. Perhaps, as in KILMARNOCK, this saint is *Ma Ernanoc* – 'my little Ernan', a seventh-century saint.

DALMENY (Lothian) 'Field on the hill'; Gaelic *dail* – 'field' and *monadh* – 'hill'.

DALMUIR (Strathclyde) 'Big field'; Gaelic *dail* – 'field' and *mor* – 'big', which has been confused with English 'moor' and Scots 'muir'.

DALNASPIDAL (Tayside) 'Hospice field'; Gaelic *dail* – 'field' and *spidal* – 'hospital, hospice'.

DALRYMPLE (Strathclyde) 'Field on the curving stream; Gaelic *dail* – 'field', *chruimm* – 'curved' and *puill* – 'stream, pool'.

DALZIEL (Strathclyde) Pronounced 'Dalyell'. 'White field'; Gaelic *dail* – 'field' and *geal* – 'white'.

DARNICK (Borders) 'Hidden village'; Old English *derne* – 'hidden' and *wic* – 'village, dwelling'.

DECHMONT (Lothian) 'Fine hill'; Gaelic *deagh* – 'fine' and *monadh* – 'hill'.

DEER, OLD and NEW (Grampian) Legend says: Gaelic *deur* – 'tear' because of the tears shed at the parting of St Columba and St Drostan, who founded the abbey here. More likely: Gaelic *doire* – 'forest'.

DEERNESS (Orkney) 'Door-head'; Norse *dyr* – 'door' and *nes* – 'headland', from the door-like recess in the headland.

DENNISTOUN (Strathclyde) 'Danielstown'. Old English.

DENNY (Central) 'Valley'; Old English *denu* – 'valley'.

DINGWALL (Highland) 'Plain of the meeting-place'; Norse *thing*, the Scandinavian assembly for discussion of public affairs and administration of justice, which took place at a fixed site, and *vollr* – 'plain'. The town's Gaelic name is *Bailechaul* – 'town of the cabbages'.

DOLLAR (Central) 'Poughed field'; Brittonic *dol* – 'meadow' and *ar* – 'ploughed'.

DONIBRISTLE (Fife) Could be 'clear, white fortress'; Gaelic *dun* – 'hill, fort', *brisg* – 'clear' and *gheal* – 'white', or 'fortress of Breasal', a Celtic name meaning 'warrior'.

DORNIE (Highland) 'Pebble place'; Gaelic *dornach*. DORNOCH (Highland) has the same meaning and derivation.

DOUGLAS (Strathclyde) 'Dark stream'; Gaelic *dubh glais*.

DRONGAN (Strathclyde) Gaelic *dronnan* – 'little ridge'.

34 DRUM (Tayside) 'Ridge'; Gaelic *druim* – 'back', 'ridge'.

Dryburgh

DRUMCHAPEL (Strathclyde) 'Mare's back'; Gaelic *druim* – 'back' and *capall* – 'mare'.

DRUMLANRIG (Dumfries & Galloway) 'Ridge of the clearing'; Gaelic *druim* – 'ridge' and Brittonic *llanerch* – 'clearing'.

DRUMLITHIE (Grampian) 'Grey ridge'; Gaelic *druim* – 'ridge' and *liath* – 'grey, blue'.

DRUMMOND (Highland) 'Ridge'; Gaelic *druimmain*.

DRUMNADROCHIT (Highland) 'Ridge of the bridge'; Gaelic *druim* – 'ridge' and *na drochaid* – 'of the bridge'.

DRYBURGH (Borders) 'Dry fort'; Old English *drygge* – 'dry' and *borg* – 'fort'.

DRYMEN (Central) 'Ridge'; Gaelic *druimmain*. See DRUMMOND.

DUFFTOWN (Grampian) Named after the Clan Duff, a local family.

DUMBARTON (Strathclyde) 'Hill of the Britons'; Gaelic *dun Breatuin*. The Britons themselves called the place *Alclut* – 'rock of Clyde', referring to Dumbarton Rock. The spelling of the county as Dunbartonshire was a recent, somewhat illogical, alteration.

DUMFRIES (Dumfries & Galloway) 'Hill of the copse'; Gaelic *dun* – 'hill' and *phreas* – 'copse'.

35

DUNBAR (Lothian) 'Fort on the height'; Gaelic *dun* – 'fort' and *barr* – 'height, top'.

DUNBLANE (Central) 'Hill of Blann', who was head of the monastery here c600; Gaelic *dun* – 'hill'.

DUNCANSBY (Highland) 'Village of Donald'; Norse name *Dungal* and *byr* – 'village'.

DUNDEE (Tayside) 'Hill of Deagh'; Gaelic *dun* – 'hill, fort'.

DUNFERMLINE (Fife) Perhaps 'fort on the hillock'; Gaelic *dun* – 'fort' and *meallain* – 'hillock'.

DUNLOP (Strathclyde) 'Hill of the bend'; Gaelic *dun* – 'hill' and *luib* – 'bend'.

DUNNOTTAR (Grampian) 'Castle on the sand-bank'; Gaelic *dun* – 'fort, castle' and *oitir* – 'sand-bank, reef'.

DUNOON (Strathclyde) 'Hill on the water'; Gaelic *dun* – 'hill, fort' and *obhainn* – 'water'.

DUNSINANE (Tayside) 'Hill of the breasts'; Gaelic *dun* – 'hill' and *sineachan* – 'breast'.

DURISDEER (Dumfries & Galloway) 'Door of the forest'; Gaelic *dorus* – 'door' and *doire* – 'forest'.

DURNESS (Highland) 'Deer cape'; Norse *dyr* – 'deer' and *nes* – 'cape'.

DYCE (Grampian) 'South'; Gaelic *deas*.

DYSART (Fife) 'Desert, hermit's cell, church'; Gaelic *diseart*.

EAGLESHAM (Strathclyde) Gaelic *eaglis* – 'church' and English *ham* – 'village'.

EARLSFERRY (Fife) Named after the MacDuffs, Earls of Fife. The ferry went across the Firth of Forth to North Berwick.

ECCLEFECHAN (Dumfries & Galloway) 'Church of St Fiachan'; Gaelic *eaglis* – 'church'.

ECCLESMACHAN (Lothian) 'Church of St Machan'; Gaelic *eaglis*.

Elrig

EDAY (Orkney) 'Isthmus isle'; Norse *eid* – 'isthmus' and *ey* – 'island'.

EDINBURGH (Lothian) Perhaps 'castle on the hill-slope'; Old Gaelic name was 'Dunedin'; Gaelic *dun* – 'castle, hill' and *aodann* – 'face, slope'. However, the 'Edin' part of the name may be pre-Celtic, and is very difficult to interpret. The Anglified name, Edinburgh, is influenced by the name of King Edwin of Northumbria c613. Also called 'Castle of the Maidens'.

EDNAM (Borders) 'Village of the River Eden'; 'Eden' and Old English *ham* – 'village'.

EIGG (Highland) 'Notch, notched island'; Gaelic *eag* – 'notch'.

EILEAN DONAN (Highland) 'Island of St Donan'; Gaelic *eilean* – 'island'.

ELGIN (Grampian) 'Little Ireland'; *Elg* is a poetic name for Ireland.

ELGOL (Highland, Skye) 'Enclosure of the stranger'; Gaelic *fal* – 'enclosure, fence' and *ghaill* – 'stranger'.

ELPHINSTONE (Lothian) Town of 'Alpin' one of the Pictish kings.

ELRIG (Dumfries & Galloway) 'Deer-trap, pass where deer were caught'; Gaelic *eileirg*.

ENNOCHDHU (Tayside) 'Black marsh'; Gaelic *eanach* – 'marsh' and *dubh* – 'black'.

ERIBOLL (Highland) 'Farm on the isthmus'; Norse *eid* – 'isthmus' and *bolstadr* – 'farm'.

EVANTON (Highland) Named c1800 after Evan Fraser of Balcony.

EYEMOUTH (Borders) 'Mouth of the River Eye'; perhaps from Old English *ea* – 'river'.

FAIR ISLE (Shetland) Formerly Norse *Fridarey* – 'Isle of Peace'. May now be from Norse *faer* – 'sheep'.

FALKIRK (Central) Formerly Gaelic *eaglis breac* – 'speckled church'; became Scottish *faw* – 'speckled' and *kirk*.

FALKLAND (Fife) 'Land for hawking'; Old English *fealca* – 'falcon'.

FAULDHOUSE (Lothian) 'House of the fold'; Old English *fald* – 'fold, fallow land'.

FENWICK (Strathclyde) 'Marshland farm'; Old English *fenn* – 'mud, marsh' and *wic* – 'farm'.

FETTERCAIRN (Grampian) 'Wooded slope'; Gaelic *foithir* – 'slope' and Brittonic *cardden* – 'wood'.

FINDHORN (Grampian) Named after River Findhorn; Gaelic *fionn earn* – 'white earn'. 'Earn' is an old river name, of obscure origin.

FINDOCHTY (Grampian) 'White land'; Gaelic *fionn* – 'white' and *dabhoch* – 'a measure of land'. The local pronunciation is 'Finechty' and the name is thought to have been spelled with an 'e' until a mis-spelling on a railway sign caused the present spelling to be widely accepted.

FINTRY (Central and Grampian) 'White house'; Gaelic *fionn* – 'white' and Brittonic *tref* – 'house, home'.

FOCHABERS (Grampian) 'Lake marsh'; Brittonic *fothach* – 'lake' and *abor* – 'marsh'.

FORFAR (Tayside) 'Slope of watching'; Gaelic *foithir* – 'slope' and *faire* – 'watching'.

FORRES (Grampian) 'Border-place'; Gaelic *foir* – 'border'.

FORT AUGUSTUS (Highland) So named 1730 by General Wade after William Augustus, Duke of Cumberland. Original name was *Cilcumein* – 'Church of St Cummein'. FORT GEORGE (Highland) was named after George II, in 1748, and FORT WILLIAM (Highland) was named after William of Orange in 1690. All three forts, Augustus, George and William, were built to maintain order in the Highlands.

FORTH (Strathclyde) 'Ford'; Scottish. The name of the River Forth (Lothian/Fife) is probably pre-Celtic, and may mean 'slow stream'.

FORTROSE (Highland) 'Lower cape'; Gaelic *foter* – 'under' and *ros* – 'cape'.

FOULA (Shetland) 'Bird isle'; Norse *fugl* – 'bird' and *ey* – 'island'.

FOYERS (Highland) 'A slope'; Gaelic *foithir*. Gaelic name is *eas na smuid* – 'fall of the spray'.

FRASERBURGH (Grampian) Formerly 'Faithlie'. Re-named when land bought by Sir Alexander Fraser of Phillorth, 1592. Known locally as 'The Broch', Old Scottish for 'burgh'.

FRIOCKHEIM (Tayside) Pronounced 'Freakem'. 'Land of Friock'; Scottish *freck* – 'quick, ready'. The German *heim* – 'home' was added by the owner c1830, who had lived in Germany.

FYVIE (Grampian) 'Track'; Gaelic *fiamh*, and *ie* locative ending.

GAIRLOCH (Highland) 'Short loch'; Gaelic *gearr* – 'short'. GARELOCH (Strathclyde) has the same meaning and derivation, and the village of GARELOCHHEAD on its banks, is self-explanatory.

GALASHIELS (Borders) 'Huts by the River Gala'; Scottish *shiel* – 'shieling'.

GANAVAN BAY (Strathclyde) 'Sandy beach'; Gaelic *gaineamh* – 'sand'.

GARGUNNOCK (Central) 'Pointed enclosure'; Gaelic *gear-raidh* – 'wall, garden, enclosure' and *guineach* – 'pointed'.

GARIOCH (Grampian) 'Rough place'; Gaelic *garbhach*.

GARRYNAHINE (Western Isles, Lewis) 'Pasture by the river'; Gaelic *gearraidh* – 'outer pasture' and *na h'aibhne* – 'by the river'.

GARSCADDEN (Strathclyde) 'Herring-yard'; Gaelic *gart* – 'field', *garradh* – 'garden' and *sgadan* – 'herring'.

GARTCOSH (Strathclyde) 'Yard of the cave'; Gaelic *gart* – 'field' and *cois* – 'cave'.

GARTMORE (Central) 'Big garden'; Gaelic *garradh* – 'garden, enclosed land' and *mor* – 'big'.

GARVE (Highland) 'Rough'; Gaelic *garbh*.

GIFFNOCK (Strathclyde) 'Little ridge'; Brittonic *cefn* – 'ridge' and '-ock' diminutive suffix.

GIRVAN (Strathclyde) 'Short river'; Gaelic *gearr* – 'short' and *abhainn* – 'river'.

GLAMIS (Tayside) 'Open country'; Gaelic *glamhus*.

GLASGOW (Strathclyde) 'Green hollow'; Brittonic *glas* – 'green' and *cau* – 'hollow'.

GLENCOE (Highland) 'Narrow glen'; Gaelic *caol* or *cumhann* – 'narrow'.

GLENEAGLES (Tayside) 'Glen of the church'; Gaelic *eaglis* – 'church'.

GLENFINNAN (Highland) 'Fingon's glen'. There was a fourteenth-century abbot of Iona called Fingon.

GORDONSTOWN and GORDONSTOUN (Grampian) Named after Sir Robert Gordon, who bought the Elgin estate, 1638.

GOREBRIDGE (Lothian) 'Bridge at the gore'; Old English *gara* – 'triangular piece of land'.

GOUROCK (Strathclyde) 'Goat-place'; Gaelic *gobhar* – 'goat'.

GOVAN (Strathclyde) 'Little hill'; Gaelic *gobheinn*.

GRANGEMOUTH (Central) Refers to mouth of Grange Burn. The burn is so called because it flowed past a part of Newbattle Abbey called 'Abbot's Grange'.

GRANTOWN ON SPEY (Highland) Town of the Grant family, local landowners, on River Spey. Formerly FREUCHIE.

GREENOCK (Strathclyde) 'Sunny hillock'; Gaelic *grianan* – from *grian* – 'sun'.

GRETNA (Dumfries & Galloway) Known in 1223 as 'Gretenho' – 'great hollow'; Old English *holh* – 'hollow', now contracted to *-a*.

GRUINARD (Highland) 'Green bay'; Norse *groenn* – 'green' and *fjord* – 'bay'.

HADDINGTON (Lothian) 'Hading's village'; Old English *tun* – 'village'.

HALBEATH (Fife) 'Wood of birches'; Gaelic *coille* – 'wood' and *beithe* – 'birch'.

HAMILTON (Strathclyde) Old name was 'Cadyow'. Appears to have been named c1266, after William de Hamyll, who lived here.

HARRIS (Western Isles) 'High island'; Norse *har* – 'high'.

HATTON (Grampian) 'Hall town', where the farmer or owner lived.

HAWICK (Borders) 'Hedge farm'; Old English *haga* – 'hedge' and *wic* – 'farm'.

HELENSBURGH (Strathclyde) Founded 1776 by Sir James Colquhoun, and named after his wife.

HELMSDALE (Highland) 'Hjalmund's dale'; Norse.   41

Holyrood

HOLYROOD (Lothian) 'Abbey of the Holy Cross'; Old English *rod* – 'rod, cross'.

HOPEMAN (Grampian) Founded 1805. 'High hill'; French *haut mont*.

HOUSTON (Strathclyde) 'Village of Hugo'; Old English *tun*. Refers to a Norman, Hugo de Paduinan, 1160.

HOY (Orkney) 'High island'; Norse *ha* – 'high and *ey* 'island'.

HUNTINGTOWER (Tayside) Hunting seat of Lord Ruthven.

HUNTLY (Grampian) Named by the Earl of Huntly, after a Berwickshire hamlet. Means 'hunting meadow'; Old English.

IBROX (Strathclyde) 'Ford of the badger'; Gaelic *ath* – 'ford' and *bruic* – 'badger'.

INCH (Lothian and Grampian) 'Island, meadow'; Gaelic *inis*. INSH (Highland) and INSCH (Grampian) have the same meaning and derivation.

INCHAFFRAY (Tayside) 'Isle of the offering, of mass'; Gaelic *inis* – 'island' and *aifreann* – 'mass'. This may have been land given to the Church.

INCHNADAMPH (Highland) 'Pasture of the ox'; Gaelic *inis* – 'island, pasture' and *na damh* – 'of the ox'.

INCHTAVANNACH (Strathclyde) 'Island of the monks'; Gaelic *inis* and *mhanaich* – 'monk'. Also called INCH DEVANNOC, with a similar meaning.

INNERLEITHEN (Borders) 'Mouth of the River Leithen'; Gaelic *inbhir* – 'river-mouth, confluence'.

INVERARAY (Strathclyde) At the mouth of the River Aray; Gaelic *inbhir*.

INVERBERVIE (Grampian) 'At the mouth of the River Bervie'; Gaelic *inbhir*. The town was originally called 'Aberbervie', until the Brittonic *aber* was translated into Gaelic.

INVERGORDON (Highland) Named after Sir Alexander Gordon, c1760. Formerly 'Inverbreckie'; Gaelic *breac* – 'speckled'. 'Mouth of the speckled river'.

INVERKEITHING (Fife) 'Mouth of the Keithing burn'.

INVERMORISTON (Highland) 'Mouth of the River Moriston'; *moriston* means 'big waterfalls'; Gaelic *mor* – 'big' and *easan* – 'waterfalls'.

INVERNESS (Highland) 'Mouth of the River Ness'; 'Ness' may be Old Celtic 'roaring river'.

INVERURIE (Grampian) 'Mouth of the River Urie' where it joins the River Don.

IONA (Strathclyde) Origin obscure. In earliest references it is known as 'Hi' or 'I', perhaps Norse for 'yew-place'. The 'Iona' spelling is thought to be a scribe's error, a mis-spelling of 'Ioua', or even a confusion in the manuscript with the biblical character Jonah. It is known in Gaelic as *Icolmkill* – 'island of the church of St Columba'.

IRVINE (Strathclyde) Named after the River Irvine.

ISLAY (Strathclyde) 'Ile's island'; Norse *ey* – 'island'.

JEDBURGH (Borders) 'Farm on the River Jed'; Old English *worth* – 'farm, enclosed village', which became 'burgh'.

JOHN O'GROATS (Highland) Said to be named after a man who lived here. 'Groats' may refer to coins, or to Norse *griot* – 'pebble'.

JOPPA (Lothian) Named after Joppa in Palestine c1780.

JURA (Strathclyde) 'Island of Doirad'; Gaelic *eilean* – 'island' and the personal name. 'Deer island'; Norse *dyr* – 'deer' and *ey*, is a possible alternative, although Norse names are rare in Jura.

KEITH (Grampian) 'A wood'; Brittonic *coed* – 'wood'.

KEMNAY (Grampian) 'Head of the plain'; Gaelic *ceann* – 'head' and *magh* – 'plain'.

KENMORE (Highland and Tayside) 'Big head'; Gaelic *ceann* – 'head' and *mor* – 'big'.

KENNOWAY (Fife) 'Head, main field'; Gaelic *ceann* and *achadh* – 'field'.

KETTINS (Tayside) 'Soldier place'; Gaelic *cathan* – 'soldier'.

KIELLS (Strathclyde) 'Church'; Gaelic *cill* and English plural.

KILBIRNIE (Strathclyde) 'Church of St Brendan'; Gaelic *cill*. Nearby is Birnie's Well, perhaps another reference to this saint.

KILBOWIE (Strathclyde) 'Yellow hill-back'; Gaelic *cul* – 'back' and *buidhe* – 'yellow'.

KILBRIDE, WEST and EAST (Strathclyde) 'Church of St Bride' or St Bridget; Gaelic *cill* – 'church'.

KILCREGGAN (Strathclyde) 'Church on the little crag'; Gaelic *cill* – 'church' and *creagan* – 'little crag'.

KILDONAN (Highland, Strathclyde and Western Isles, South Uist) 'Church of St Donan'; Gaelic *cill* – 'church'. St Donan was martyred at Eigg in AD 617.

KILDRUMMY (Grampian) 'Wood on the ridge'; Gaelic *coille* – 'wood' and *druim* – 'ridge'.

44 KILLEAN (Strathclyde) 'Church of St John'; Gaelic *Iain*.

KILLIECRANKIE (Tayside) 'Wood of the aspens'; Gaelic *coille* – 'wood' and *critheann* – 'aspen'. In Gaelic, called 'battle of Rory's meadow' – *cath raon Ruaraidh*.

KILLIN (Central) 'White church'; Gaelic *cill* – 'church' and *fionn* – 'white'.

KILMACOLM (Strathclyde) 'Church of my Colm' – St Columba; Gaelic *cill* – 'church'.

KILMARNOCK (Strathclyde) 'Church of little Ernan' – St Ernan; Gaelic *cill* – 'church'.

KILMARTIN (Strathclyde) 'Church of St Martin of Tours'; Gaelic *cill* – 'church'.

KILSYTH (Strathclyde) 'Church of the arrows'; Gaelic *cill* – 'church' and *saighde* – 'arrow'.

KILWINNING (Strathclyde) 'Church of St Finnan'; from the Brittonic form of the name, Wynnin. St Finnan was a great sixth-century Irish saint.

KINCARDINE (Fife) 'At the head of the wood'; Gaelic *cinn* – 'head' and Brittonic *cardden* – 'wood, thicket'. KINCARDINE O'NEILL (Grampian) is on land which belonged to the ancient O'Neill family of Northern Ireland.

KINCRAIG (Highland) 'At the head of the rock'; Gaelic *cinn* – 'at the head' and *creag* – 'rock, crag'.

Killin

KING EDWARD (Grampian) 'At the head of the division'; Gaelic *cinn* – 'at the head' and *sadaradh* – 'division'. The present name is a folk-etymology.

KINGHORN (Fife) 'At the head of the marsh'; Gaelic *cinn* – 'at the head' and *gronn* – 'marsh'.

KINGUSSIE (Highland) Pronounced 'Kinyoosie'. 'At the head of the fir-wood'; Gaelic *cinn* – 'at the head' and *guibhas* – 'fir-tree'.

KINLOCH (Tayside) 'At the head of the loch'; Gaelic *cinn* – 'at the head' and 'loch'. **KINLOCHLEVEN** (Highland) is at the head of Loch Leven.

KINLOSS (Grampian) 'Height, headland, of herbs'; Gaelic *ceann* – 'head' and *lossa* – 'herbs'.

KINNEIL (Central) 'At the head of the wall'; Gaelic *cinn* – 'at the head' and *fhabhail* – 'wall', perhaps the Antonine Wall, built by the Romans to the north of Hadrian's Wall.

KINROSS (Tayside) 'At the head of the cape'; Gaelic *cinn* – 'at the head' and *ros* – 'cape'.

KINTAIL (Highland) 'At the head of the salt-water'; Gaelic *cinn* – 'at the head' and *t'saile* – 'of the salt-water'.

KINTORE (Grampian) 'At the head of the hill'; Gaelic *cinn* – 'at the head' and *torr* – 'hill'.

KINTYRE (Strathclyde) 'At the head of the land'; Gaelic *cinn* – 'at the head' and *tir* – 'land'.

KIPPEN (Central) 'Little stump'; Gaelic *ceap* – 'a stump' and the diminutive *-an*.

KIRKCALDY (Fife) 'Fort on the hard hill'; Brittonic *caer* – 'fort', *caled* – 'hard' and *din* – 'hill-fort'. *Caer* has now become 'Kirk-'.

KIRKCOLM (Dumfries & Galloway) 'Church of St Columba'.

KIRKCUDBRIGHT (Dumfries & Galloway) 'Church of St Cuthbert', a seventh-century Northumbrian monk.

KIRKINTILLOCH (Strathclyde) 'Hill-head fort'; Brittonic *caer* or Gaelic *cathair* – 'fort', *cinn* – 'at the head' and *tulaich* – 'of the hill'.

KIRRIEMUIR (Tayside) 'Big quarter'; Gaelic *ceathramh* – 'quarter' and *mor* – 'big'. Refers to a piece of land, a quarter of a davoch in size. The davoch was a variable measure of land about enough to support a household.

KISHORN (Highland) 'Big cape'; Norse *keis horn*.

KNOCK (Many) 'Hill'; Gaelic *cnoc*.

KNOCKANDO (Grampian) 'Market hill'; Gaelic *cnoc* – 'hill' and *cheannachd* – 'market'.

KNOYDART (Highland) 'Cnut's fjord, sea-loch'; Norse.

KYLEAKIN (Highland) 'Straits of Haakon', King of Norway; Gaelic *caol* – 'strait'.

LADYBANK (Fife) 'Moist slope'; Gaelic *leathad* – 'slope' and *bog* – 'soft, moist'. The monks of Lindores dug peats here in the thirteenth century, and it was called 'Our Lady's bog'. In the nineteenth century it was 'improved' to Ladybank.

LAGGAN (Highland) 'Little hollow'; Gaelic *lagan*.

LAIRG (Highland) 'A plain'; Gaelic *learg*.

LANARK (Strathclyde) 'Forest glade'; Brittonic *llanerch*. LANRICK (Central) has the same meaning and derivation.

LANGHOLM (Dumfries & Galloway) 'Long meadow'; Norse *holm* – 'meadow'.

LARBERT (Central) 'House by the wood'; Gaelic *larach* – 'house', usually, in modern Gaelic, a ruined house and Brittonic *perth* – 'wood, thicket'. The first element may originally have been Gaelic *leth* – 'half, portion'.

LARGS (Strathclyde) 'Plain, hillside'; Gaelic *learg* with English plural.

LASSWADE (Lothian) 'Ford on the meadow'; Old English *laes woed*.

East Linton

LATHERON (Highland) 'Fork of a river'; Gaelic *laghran*. LATHERONWHEEL (Highland) is 'Pool at the river fork'; Gaelic *poll* – 'pool'.

LAURENCEKIRK (Grampian) 'Church of St Laurentius', a third-century martyr.

LEADHILLS (Strathclyde) From the lead which was mined here from the Middle Ages.

LEITH (Lothian) Stands on the Water of Leith, perhaps from Brittonic *llaith* – 'moist'.

LENZIE (Strathclyde) 'Wet plain'; Gaelic *leana*.

LERWICK (Shetland) 'Mud bay'; Norse *leir* – 'mud' and *vik* – 'bay'.

LESLIE (Fife) 'Holly garden'; Brittonic *llys* – 'garden, enclosure' and *celyn* – 'holly'.

LESMAHAGOW (Strathclyde) 'Church of St Fechin'; Gaelic *eaglis* – 'church' and the name of the saint in its diminutive form 'Ma-Fhergu'. St Fechin lived in the seventh century.

LETTERFEARN (Highland) 'Slope with the alders'; Gaelic *leitir* – 'slope', usually with many springs and streams, and *fearn* – 'alder'. There are other place-names containing the 'letter' element, such as LETTERFINLAY (Highland), which is the land on the slope which belonged to Finlay.

LEUCHARS (Fife) 'Place of rushes'; Gaelic *luachair* – 'rushes'.

LEWIS (Western Isles) 'Marshy place'; Gaelic *leoig* – 'marsh'. Alternatively, it may be 'house of song'; Norse *ljod* – 'song' and *hus* – 'house'.

LINCLUDEN (Dumfries & Galloway) 'Pool on the River Cluden'; Brittonic *llyn* – 'lake'.

LINLITHGOW (Lothian) 'Lake by the wet hollow'; Brittonic *llyn* – 'lake', *llaith* – 'wet' and *cau* – 'hollow'. There is repetition of ideas in this name.

LINTON, EAST and WEST (Lothian) (Borders) 'Flax field'; Old English *lin* –'flax' and *tun* – 'field, enclosure, house'.

LINWOOD (Strathclyde) 'Wood by the lake'; Brittonic *llyn* – 'lake'.

LOANHEAD (Lothian) 'At the head or end of the lane'; Scottish.

LOCHALSH (Highland) 'Foaming lake'; Gaelic *ailseach*.

LOCHARBRIGGS (Dumfries & Galloway) 'Bridges over the rushes'; Gaelic *luachair* – 'rushes'.

LOCHGELLY (Fife) 'Place by the white loch'; Gaelic *geal* – 'white'.

LOCHINVAR (Dumfries & Galloway) 'Loch on the height'; Gaelic *barr* – 'height'.

LOCHINVER (Highland) 'Place at the loch-mouth'; Gaelic *inbhir* – 'river-mouth, confluence'.

LOCHNAGAR (Grampian) 'Loch of the outcrop'; Gaelic *gaire* – 'outcrop'.

LOCHWINNOCH (Strathclyde) 'Loch of St Wynnin', the Brittonic form of St Finnan.

LOCKERBIE (Dumfries & Galloway) 'Locard's house'; Norse *byr* – 'house, village'.

LOMOND, WEST (Fife) 'Beacon'; Brittonic *lluman*. LOCH LOMOND and BEN LOMOND (Strathclyde), and the LOMOND HILLS (Fife) have the same derivation.

49

LONGNIDDRY (Lothian) 'Land of Niddrie'; Gaelic *lann* – 'land'.

LORN (Strathclyde) Named after Loarn, one of the sons of Erc, who were the first Gaelic settlers in Scotland.

LOSSIEMOUTH (Grampian) 'Mouth of the River Lossie'. Lossie may mean 'river with many plants'; Gaelic *lus* – 'herb'.

LOTHIAN 'Land of Leodonus'.

LUCE, OLD and NEW (Dumfries & Galloway) Gaelic *lus* – 'herb'. LUSS (Strathclyde) has the same meaning and derivation.

LUMPHANAN (Grampian) 'Land of St Finnan'; Gaelic *lann* – 'land'. A church in this village is dedicated to St Finnan.

LUNDIN LINKS (Fife) 'Wet plain'; Gaelic *leana* and Scottish 'links'.

MACDUFF (Grampian) Named by James Duff, Earl of Fife, 1783

MACHRIHANISH (Strathclyde) 'Plain by the high cape'; Gaelic *machair* – 'plain' and Norse *har* – 'high' and *nes* – 'cape, promontory'.

MAGGIEKNOCKATER (Grampian) 'Field of the fuller'; Gaelic *magh* – 'field', *an fhucadair* – 'of the fuller'.

MAINLAND (Orkney and Shetland) From Norse *Meginland* – 'main, principal island'. These are the biggest islands of the Orkneys and Shetlands.

MALLAIG (Highland) 'Bay of gulls'; Norse *mar* – 'gull' and *vik* – 'bay'.

MARKINCH (Fife) 'Horse meadow'; Gaelic *marc* – 'horse' and *inis* – 'island, meadow'.

MARYBURGH (Highland) Named after Queen Mary, wife of William III c1690.

MARYHILL (Strathclyde) Named after Mary Hill of Garbraid, the owner of the land c1760.

MAUCHLINE (Strathclyde) 'Plain with the pool'; Gaelic *magh* – 'plain' and *linn* – 'pool'.

MAUD (Grampian) Named after the Oldmaud Estate, which is from Gaelic *allt madaidh* – 'burn of the dog, wolf or fox'.

MAYBOLE (Strathclyde) 'Plain of danger'; Gaelic *magh* – 'plain' and *baoghail* – 'danger'.

MEARNS (Tayside) 'Land of the steward'; Gaelic *maor* – 'steward'. NEWTON MEARNS (Strathclyde) is similar. A royal steward of Scotland was the founder of the great line of Stuart kings.

MELROSE (Borders) 'Bare moor'; Gaelic *maol* – 'bare' and *ros* – 'moor'.

MENTEITH (Central) 'Moor of the River Teith'; Gaelic *moire* – 'moor'.

MERKLAND POINT (Strathclyde) There are many Merk-lands in Scotland, and the name means land rented at a cost of a Merk, which was two-thirds of a Scots Pound.

METHIL (Fife) 'Soft wood'; Gaelic *maoth* – 'soft' and *coille*– 'wood'. METHLICK (Grampian) has a similar meaning and derivation.

MEY (Highland) 'Place in the plain'; Gaelic *magh* – 'plain'.

MILNGAVIE (Strathclyde) 'Windmill'; Gaelic *muileann* – 'mill' and *goath* – 'wind'. Should be pronounced 'Mulgay'.

MOFFAT (Dumfries & Galloway) 'Long plain'; Gaelic *magh* – 'plain' and *fada* – 'long'.

MONADHLIATH (Highland) 'Grey-blue ridge'; Gaelic *monadh* – 'moor, ridge' and *liath* – 'grey blue'. Pronounced 'Monachlee'.

MONCRIEFF (Tayside) 'Ridge with the trees'; Gaelic *monadh* – 'moor, ridge' and *craobhe* – 'tree'.

MONIFIETH (Tayside) 'Moor with the bog'; Gaelic *moine* – 'moor' and *feith* – 'bog'.

MONTROSE (Tayide) 'Moor on the headland'; Gaelic *moine* – 'peat, moor' and *ros* – 'headland'.

MONYMUSK (Grampian) 'Muddy bog'; Gaelic *moine* – 'peat, bog' and *musgach* – 'muddy'.

MORAR (Highland) 'Big water'; Gaelic *mor* – 'big' and *dobhar* – 'water'.

MOTHERWELL (Strathclyde) 'Well of the Mother', perhaps a reference to the Virgin Mary.

MOUNT FLORIDA (Strathclyde) Named after 'Mount Florida House', which belonged to a family from Florida, United States.

MOUNT VERNON (Strathclyde) Named after George Washington's estate in the United States.

MUCK (Highland) 'Island of pigs'; Gaelic *muc* – 'pig'.

MUCKLE FLUGGA (Shetland) 'Big precipices'; Norse *mykill* – 'big' and *flugga* – 'precipices'.

MUIR OF ORD (Highland) 'Moor with the steep hill'; Gaelic *ord* – 'steep, round hill'.

MULL (Strathclyde) Probably 'bare hill'; Gaelic *maol* – 'bare top, brow of a cape', but not certain. May also be from Gaelic *muilead* – 'dear, beloved'.

MUSSELBURGH (Lothian) 'Mussel town'. Sea food has been a product of the town since the eleventh century, and probably even earlier.

NAIRN (Highland) From the River Nairn. Formerly Invernairn – mouth of the River Nairn. The meaning of the river name is obscure.

NEMPHLAR (Strathclyde) 'Sacred ground'; Gaelic *neimhidh* – 'church land' and *lar* – 'ground'.

NEVIS (Highland) From the River Nevis, which is probably from an Old Celtic word for water. Other interpretations of the name of Scotland's highest mountain are that it is from the Gaelic for 'without beauty' or the Old Irish for 'venomous one'. Similar uncomplimentary references to this mountain appear throughout Gaelic literature, and are evi-

Oban

dence of the fear which this great mountain aroused.

NEWBATTLE (Lothian) 'New house'; Old English *neowe* – 'new' and *botl* – 'house'.

NEWBURGH (Grampian and Fife) 'New dwelling, village'; Old English *burg* – 'town, village', often fortified. The Newburgh in Fife was probably founded as early as the twelfth century — its name is no longer very appropriate. NEWSTEAD (Borders) and NEWTON (Several) have a similar meaning.

NEWMACHAR (Grampian) Probably from Gaelic *machair* – 'a plain, flat space', although there has long been a traditional connection with St Machar, a disciple of St Columba, who travelled and established churches in the area.

NEWTONMORE (Highland) 'New town on the moor'; English.

NIDDRIE (Lothian) 'New town'; Brittonic *newydd* – 'new' and *tref* – 'town, hamlet'.

NITSHILL (Strathclyde) 'Hill with the nuts'; Scottish 'nit' – 'a nut'.

OBAN (Strathclyde) 'Little bay'; Gaelic *ob* and the diminutive ending *-an*.

OCHILTREE (Strathclyde) 'High house'; Brittonic *uchel* – 'high' and *tref* – 'house, town'.

OGILVIE (Tayside) 'High place'; Brittonic *uchel* – 'high' and *fa* – 'plain, place'.

OLDMELDRUM (Grampian) 'Bare ridge'; Gaelic *maol* – 'bare' and *druim* – 'ridge', with English 'old'.

ORKNEY 'Whale isles'; Norse *orc* – 'whale' and *ey* – 'island'. The adjective 'Orcadian' is derived from the earliest literary references to the name in a Greek-influenced form *Orcades*.

OXGANGS (Lothian) A grant of land, as much as an ox could plough or 'gang' – Scottish.

OXNAM (Borders) 'Village of the oxen'; Old English *oxena-ham*.

OYKEL BRIDGE (Highland) Named after River Oykel, from Brittonic *uchel* – 'high', referring to the banks of the river. Ptolemy in the twelfth century called it *Ripa Alta* – 'high banks' in Latin.

PAISLEY (Strathclyde) 'Pasture slope'; Brittonic *pasgell* – 'pasture' and *llethr* – 'slope'.

PATNA (Strathclyde) So named c1810 after Patna on the Ganges in India, where the former Laird made his fortune.

PEEBLES (Borders) 'Tent'; Brittonic *pebyll*.

PENICUIK (Lothian) 'Hill of the cuckoo'; Brittonic *penn* – 'head, hill' and *cog* – 'cuckoo'.

PENNINGHAME (Dumfries & Galloway) 'Penny holding'; land rented for one penny.

PERTH (Tayside) 'Thicket, wood'; Brittonic *perth*. The town was also called 'St Johnstoun', probably after the church here dedicated to St John the Baptist. The local football team bears this name.

PETERHEAD (Grampian) Promontory of St Peter. The ancient Church of St Peter is still here. Formerly Inverugie – 'at the mouth of the River Ugie'. Locally known as the Blue

Toon because of the blue boot-stockings which the fishermen used to wear. They were called 'blue mogganers', from Gaelic *mogan* – 'stocking'.

PILRIG (Lothian) 'Peel ridge' i.e. ridge where a fortified tower had been built.

PITCAPLE (Grampian) 'Land of the mare'; Brittonic *pett* – 'land, share' and Gaelic *capuill* – 'mare'.

PITCOX (Lothian) 'Land of the fifth share'; Brittonic *pett* – 'land, share' and Gaelic *coig* – 'five'.

PITFOUR (Tayside) 'Pasture land'; Brittonic *pett* and Gaelic *phuir* – 'pasture'.

PITLOCHRY (Tayside) 'Stony land'; Brittonic *pett* – 'land, share' and Gaelic *cloichreach* – 'stony'. The town's Gaelic name is *Bailechlochrie*, which has the same meaning.

PITSCOTTIE (Fife) 'Land with the little flock'; Brittonic *pett* – 'land' and Gaelic *sgotan* – 'little flock'.

PITTENWEEM (Fife) 'Land with the cave'; Brittonic *pett* – 'land' and Gaelic *uamh* – 'cave'.

PLOCKTON (Highland) Gaelic *ploc* – 'large clod, turf' and English *tun* – 'village, town'.

POLLOKSHAWS (Strathclyde) 'Little pool in the woods'; Gaelic *poll* – 'pool' and Old English *scaga* – 'a wood'. POLLOKSHIELDS (Strathclyde) is 'shielings, cottages, by the little pool'. The name Polloc was adopted by a local landowner in the twelfth century, and these names may come from him, rather than from the original 'little pool'.

PORT CHARLOTTE (Strathclyde, Islay) Named in 1828 after Lady Charlotte, mother of W. F. Campbell of Islay. PORT ELLEN (Strathclyde, Islay) was named in 1821 after Lady Ellenor, his wife.

PORT GLASGOW (Strathclyde) Site feued by Glasgow Town Council c1668.

PORTKNOCKIE (Grampian) 'Harbour by the little hill'; Gaelic *cnoc* – 'hill'.

55

PORTOBELLO (Lothian) Named after a house built c1750 by a sailor who was present at the capture of Puerto Bello, Panama, c1739.

PORTREE (Highland, Skye) 'Slope by the harbour'; Gaelic *ruighe* – 'slope', often confused with *righ* – 'king' and connected with a visit of James V in 1540 to Skye.

PORTSOY (Grampian) 'Port of the warrior'; Gaelic *saoi* – 'warrior'.

PRESTONPANS (Lothian) The name refers to salt pans made here by the monks of Newbattle Abbey, for extracting salt from the sea. Preston means 'priest's town'; Old English *preost* – 'priest' and *tun* – 'village'. Again, this probably refers to the monks of the Abbey.

PRESTWICK (Strathclyde) 'Priest place'; Old English *preost* – 'priest' and *wic* – 'place, dwelling'.

QUEENSFERRY (Lothian) Queen Margaret, wife of King Malcolm Canmore, crossed here c1090, and the river crossing was named in her honour.

QUINISH (Strathclyde, Mull) 'Promontory of the sheep-fold'; Norse *koi* – 'sheep-fold' and *nes* – 'promontory'.

RAASAY (Highland, Skye) 'Roe-deer island'; Norse *rar* – 'roe-deer' and *ey* – 'island'.

RAIT (Tayside and Highland) 'Fort'; Gaelic *rath*.

RANNOCH (Highland, Strathclyde and Tayside) 'Bracken place'; Gaelic *raineach* – 'bracken'.

RATHO (Lothian) 'Place of mounds'; Brittonic *rathau* – 'mounds, hills'.

RATTRAY (Tayside) 'Farm by the fort'; Gaelic *rath* – 'fort' and Brittonic *tref* – 'farm, house'.

RENFREW (Strathclyde) 'Point of the current' referring to the confluence of the rivers Gryfe and Clyde; Brittonic *rhynfrwd*.

RESTALRIG (Lothian) 'Hall on the ridge'; Brittonic *llys* – 'hall', *tal* – 'on the' and *rhych* – 'ridge'.

RESTON (Borders) 'Farm by the brushwood'; Old English *hris* – 'brushwood' and *tun* – 'farm, village'.

RIDDRIE (Strathclyde) 'Red shieling'; Gaelic *ruadh* – 'red' and *airigh* – 'shieling'.

RONALDSAY (Orkney) NORTH RONALDSAY is the island of Ninian, or Ringan, the fourth-century saint. SOUTH RONALDSAY, however, is the island of Ronald or Rognvald, brother of a ninth-century Earl of Orkney.

ROSEHEARTY (Grampian) 'Cape of Abartach'; Gaelic *ros* – 'cape, promontory', and the Irish personal name.

ROSEMARKIE (Highland) 'Cape of the horse'; Gaelic *ros* – 'cape' and *marc* – 'horse'.

ROSYTH (Fife) 'Landing-place headland'; Gaelic *ros* – 'cape, headland' and Old English *hythe* – 'landing-place'.

ROTHESAY (Strathclyde, Bute) 'Roderick's island'; Norse *ey* – 'island'. Roderick was the son of the original landowners in Bute.

ROWARDENNAN (Central) 'Promontory of Adamnan's hill'; Gaelic *rubha* – 'promontory', *ard* – 'hill' and the saint's name, Adamnan, reduced to 'ennan'.

ROXBURGH (Borders) 'Castle of Hroc'; Old English *burh* – 'castle, town'. The personal name, Hroc, is Old English for 'the rook', probably a nickname.

RUM (Highland) Very obscure. Perhaps from Gaelic *druim* – 'hill-ridge'.

RUTHERGLEN (Strathclyde) 'Red glen, valley'; Gaelic *ruadh* – 'red'.

ST ABBS HEAD (Borders) Originally called 'Coldeburchesnead'. Named after Aebba, first Abbess of Coldingham Priory, which is nearby, c650.

St Andrews

ST ANDREWS (Fife) Named after the Church of St Andrew here, which was originally named after St Regulus, but was re-named by King Kenneth McAlpin in 850. The town's earliest name was Kilrimont — 'church at the royal hill'; Gaelic *cill* – 'church', *righ* – 'king' and *monadh* – 'hill'.

ST KILDA (Western Isles) Originally called Hirta, probably meaning 'western island', from Gaelic *iar* – 'west'. Alternatively, it may be from Norse *skilda* – 'a shield', referring to the shape of the island. The name came to be falsely associated with a saint, Kilda, who did not exist. St Kilda was cleared of its population in 1930.

ST MONANS (Fife) Named after St Monans, Bishop of Clonfert in Ireland, in 572.

SALTCOATS (Strathclyde) Cottages belonging to salt workers at the salt-pans along the coast here.

SANQUHAR (Dumfries & Galloway) 'Old fort'; Gaelic *sean* – 'old' and *cathair* – 'fort'.

SCONE (Tayside) 'Lump, mass'; Gaelic *sgonn*. Probably referring to the Mote Hill. SCOONIE (Fife) has the same meaning and derivation.

SCOTSCALDER (Highland) That part of the valley of the River Calder which was inhabited by Scots or Celts, as opposed to Norsemen.

SCRABSTER (Highland) 'Rocky farm'; Norse *sker* – 'rock' and *bolstadr* – 'farm'.

SELKIRK (Borders) 'Church by the hall'; Old English *sele* – 'hall' and *cirice* – 'church'.

SHETLAND These islands had a variety of names in the past, the most common being 'Hjaltland', which may be from the personal name *Hjalti*, or from the Norse *hjalt* – 'a hilt'. The 'Zetland' spelling is an attempt to reproduce the former pronunciation of the name as 'Yetland', and became in the late-eighteenth century the more prestigious and 'official' spelling of the name. It has since died out, and Shetland is the more widespread, and etymologically more authentic, spelling and pronunciation. The classical name, given by some Latin writers to the islands, was 'Thule', which is of obscure origin.

SKIRLING (Borders) 'Rocky torrent'; Norse *sker* – 'rock' and Old English *llynn* – 'torrent'.

SKYE (Highland) 'Wing'; Gaelic *sgiath*. Describing the shape of the island.

SLAMANNAN (Central) 'Moor of Manau'; Gaelic *sliabh* – 'moor, hill-face'.

SLEAT (Highland) 'Flat land'; Norse *sletta*.

SLIGACHAN (Highland) 'Shell-place'; Gaelic *slige* – 'shell'.

SORBIE (Dumfries & Galloway) 'Muddy farm'; Norse *saur-byr*.

STAFFA (Highland) 'Isle of the staves'; Norse *staf* – 'stave' and *ey* – 'island'. This describes the columns of basaltic rock which make up the island, and give the famous 'Fingal's cave', on the island, its distinctive appearance. Fingal is a character of Celtic legend.

STENHOUSEMUIR (Central) 'Moor of the stone house'; Old English *stan* – 'stone', *hus* – 'house' and *mor* – 'moor'.

STEWARTON (Strathclyde) Village of Walter, the High Steward of King David I, c1140.

59

STIRLING (Central) Very obscure. Possibly 'house of Velyn'; Brittonic *ystre* – 'house' and the personal name.

STONEHAVEN (Grampian) 'Stony harbour'; Norse *steinn* – 'stone' and *hofn* – 'haven, harbour'.

STORNOWAY (Western Isles) 'Steering bay'; Norse *stjorn* – 'steering' and *vagr* – 'bay'. It is not clear exactly what this refers to.

STRANRAER (Dumfries & Galloway) 'Thick point, promontory'; Gaelic *sron* – 'point, nose' and *reamhar* – 'thick'.

STRATHAVEN (Strathclyde) Pronounced 'Straven'. 'Valley of the River Avon, Avon Water'; Gaelic *srath* – 'valley'.

STRATHMIGLO (Fife) 'Valley of the pig-pen'; Gaelic *srath* – 'valley' and *muclach* – 'pig-pen'.

STROMNESS (Orkney) 'Cape in the current'; Norse *straumr* – 'current' and *nes* – 'cape, promontory'.

STRONACHLACHAR (Central) 'Cape of the mason'; Gaelic *sron* – 'cape, nose' and *a'chlachair* – 'of the mason'.

STRONTIAN (Highland) 'Beacon point'; Gaelic *sron* – 'point' and *teine* – 'fire, beacon'.

SULLOM VOE (Shetland) 'Bay of the gannets'; Norse *sule* – 'gannet' and *vagr* – 'bay'.

SUTHERLAND (Highland) 'Southern territory'; Norse *sudr* – 'southern' and *land*. So named by the Scandinavian settlers of the Northern Isles.

TAIN (Highland) Old river name of obscure, probably pre-Celtic, origin, similar to Thames, Tay, etc.

TARLAND (Grampian) 'Bull land'; Gaelic *tarbh* – 'bull' and *lann* – 'land'. TARVES (Grampian) is also from Gaelic *tarbh* and means 'bull-place'.

TAYNUILT (Strathclyde) 'House on the burn'; Gaelic *tigh* – 'house', *an uillt* – 'on the burn'.

TEMPLE (Lothian) Land which was property of the Knights Templar.

Tobermory

TERREGLES (Dumfries & Galloway) 'Village with the church'; Brittonic *tref* – 'village', *yr eglwys* – 'of the church'.

THUNDERGAY (Strathclyde, Arran) 'Windy hill'; Gaelic *torr* – 'hill' and *na gaoith* – 'of the wind'. Thought to have originally been 'backside to the wind' – *ton re gaoith*!

THURSO (Highland) After the River Thurso: 'bull river', Norse *thjorsa*.

TIGHNABRUAICH (Strathclyde) 'House on the burn'; Gaelic *tigh* – 'house' and *na bruaich* – 'on the burn'.

TILLICOULTRY (Central) 'Hill of the back-land'; Gaelic *tulach* – 'hill', *cul* – 'back' and *tir* – 'land'.

TINWALD (Dumfries & Galloway) 'Meeting place'; Norse *thingvollr*. Same as DINGWALL (Highland).

TIREE (Strathclyde) 'Land of Ith'; Gaelic *tir* – 'land'. There is no information available about the person, Ith.

TOBERMORY (Strathclyde) 'Well of Mary'; Gaelic *tobar* – 'well'. Probably refers to the Virgin Mary.

TOMINTOUL (Grampian) 'Barn-like knoll'; Gaelic *tom* – 'knoll' and *an t'sabhail* – 'of the barn'.

TONGUE (Highland) 'Spit of land'; Norse *tunga*.

TORPHINS (Grampian) 'White hill'; Gaelic *torr* – 'hill' and *fionn* – 'white'.

TRANENT (Lothian) 'Village of the streams'; Brittonic *tref* – 'village' and *naint* – 'streams'.

TROON (Strathclyde) 'Point'; Gaelic *sron* – 'nose, point'.

TULLICH (Highland) 'Hill'; Gaelic *tulach*. TULLOCH (Highland) has this derivation, too.

TULLIBODY (Central) 'Hill with the house'; Gaelic *tulach* – 'hill' and *both* – 'house'.

TYNDRUM (Central) 'House on the ridge'; Gaelic *tigh* – 'house' and *an druim* – 'on the ridge'.

UDDINGSTON (Strathclyde) 'Village of the sons of Udd'; Old English *tun* – 'village'.

UIG (Highland, Skye) 'Bay'; Gaelic *uig*.

ULLAPOOL (Highland) 'Olaf's farm'; Norse *bolstadr* – 'farm', reduced to '-pool'.

URQUHART (Grampian and Highland) 'Place at a wood'; Brittonic *air* – 'on, upon' and *cardden* – 'wood'.

VATERSAY (Western Isles) 'Glove island'; Norse *vottr* – 'glove' and *ey* – 'island'.

VOE (Shetland) 'Little bay'; Norse *vagr*.

WANLOCKHEAD (Dumfries & Galloway) 'White slab'; Brittonic *gwen* – 'white' and *llech* – 'slab, stone'.

WATERLOO (Strathclyde, Highland and Tayside) Named after the famous battle, and the Belgian village where it was fought.

WAUK MILL (Numerous examples) 'Cloth-dressing mill'; Scottish *wauk* – 'to full, dress cloth'.

WEMYSS, EAST (Fife) 'Caves'; Gaelic *uamh* – 'cave'.

WESTRAY (Orkney) 'Western island'; Norse *vestr* – 'west' and *ey* – 'island'.

WHALSAY (Shetland) 'Whale island'; Norse *hvalsey*.

WHITBURN (Lothian) 'White stream, burn'.

WICK (Highland) 'Little bay'; Norse *vik*, cognate with Gaelic *uig*.

WIGTON (Dumfries & Galloway) 'Farm village'; Old English *wic* – 'farm' and *tun* – 'village'.

WISHAW (Strathclyde) 'Wood of Wice'; Scottish 'shaw'.

WRATH, CAPE (Highland) 'Turning cape'; Norse *hvarf* – 'turning, shelter'.

YARROW (Borders) From the River Yarrow; Gaelic *garbh* – 'rough'.

YELL (Shetland) 'Barren island'; Norse *gelld* – 'barren'.

YETHOLM (Borders) 'Hamlet at the gate'; Old English *geat* – 'gate, pass' and *ham* – 'hamlet, village' or *holm* – 'meadow'.

YOKER (Strathclyde) 'Low, bottom ground'; Gaelic *iochdar* – 'bottom part'.

READING LIST

Dorward, David, *Scotland's Place-Names*, Blackwood, 1979

Fenton, Alexander, *The Various Names of Shetland*, Blackwood, 1973

Field, John, *Place-names of Great Britain and Ireland*, David & Charles, 1980

Johnston, J B, *Place-Names of Scotland*, John Murray, 1934

MacBain, Alex, *Place-Names of the Highlands and Islands of Scotland*, Eneas Mackay, 1922

MacKenzie, W C, *Scottish Place-Names*, Kegan Paul, Trench, Trubner & Co Ltd, 1931

MacKinnon, Lachlan, *Place-Names of Lochaber*, Saltire Society, 1973

Nicolaisen, W F H, *Scottish Place-Names*, Batsford, 1976

Philip, Alexander, *The Picts in Angus and their Place-Names*, Routledge, 1925

Wainwright, F T, *The Problem of the Picts*, Nelson, 1955

Place-Names on Maps of Scotland and Wales, Ordnance Survey, 1973

A Key to Highland Placenames, An Commun Gaidhealach, 1966